UNRULY BEAST

eean m. tyson

Copyright © 2019 by Eean Tyson All rights reserved.
This book or any portion thereof may not be reproduced or used in any manner whatsoever without the express written permission of the author except for the use of brief quotations in a book review. The views and opinions expressed in this book do not necessarily represent that of 310 Brown Street, its owner or employees.

Released April 2019

Printed in the United States of America
Edited By Sunni Soper
ISBN 978-0-9998291-5-8
Published by 310 Brown Street
www.310brownstreet.com
www.eeantyson.com

he remains standing,

amongst rubble and decay

hoping, to flower

Unruly Beast is the author's journey from black boy to black man encompassing his experiences and perspective. This collection of poems reveals the internal workings of a man still navigating through life and still learning to embrace all that he is and all he can be.

This is the first published collection of poems from the author, Eean M. Tyson. Writing was initially, a way for him to handle his anger in his younger years and has now become a way for him to connect with people by sharing his experiences and also the lessons he has learned along the way.

the fierce in his eyes

saliva dripping from teeth

defending his Heart

To my parents,
Thank You for opening every door
and empowering me to choose my own way

Also, to my Mom
I present, my first born

TABLE OF CONTENTS

I.

11.	SOFT
12.	ANOTHER DAY
13.	ALL SMILES
14.	LONELY ROAD
15.	SELF
19.	WRITING
20.	LETTING GO
21.	MIND/HEART
22.	PROTECT
23.	ALL I HEAR
24.	FIST
25.	STILL LEARNING
26.	MY SILENCE
27.	MASCULINITY
28.	I HAVE KNOWN
29.	WHEN YOUR PEN GOES SILENT
32.	SHARDS
34.	STILLNESS
35.	FIRE
36.	ONCE

II.

37.	ROAD TRIP
38.	TO LOVE ME
39.	LOVE LANGUAGE
40.	INTRIGUE
41.	DOWN THE SLIDE
42.	KISS ME
43.	CLING
44.	SIMUTANEOUSLY
45.	A LOVER'S LIE
48.	BLACK WOMAN
52.	MEMORY
55.	SHEETS OF MUSIC
57.	AMUSEMENT PARK
58.	A BROKEN PROMISE
61.	ALL THAT MATTERS
64.	ALTERING SKYLINES
65.	MAGIC
69.	DATING SUCKS

III.

74.	SNEAKERHEAD
79.	MY BLACK SKIN
80.	BEARD
84.	BACK IN THE DAY
87.	COLORBLIND
90.	NEVER DIED
93.	INSTRUMENT OF PRAISE
95.	6 HOURS
95.	IF THERE BE HEAVEN
99.	A WISE MAN
102.	MY MOTHER

SOFT

I —

Am no soft place

This world
Has yet to allow me the space
to learn softness;

Only to hope;

To one day be

Bulletproof.

ANOTHER DAY

Most days,

My eyes open before

Morning rises from the horizon,

It is then—

I find all the reasons

I deserve,

Another day

ALL SMILES

The smile—

Is the only
Facial expression
I have been able to master.

Therefore,

I am usually,
All smiles
or,

Nothing at all

LONELY ROAD

my smile is

a lonely crooked road

usually admired

but

rarely traveled

SELF

"A lack of transparency results in distrust and a deep sense of insecurity"

                                        The Dali Lama

Self—

I haven't been honest with you,
Been lying for so long,
Not sure I could recognize truth if it were
Staring at me in the mirror,

It is said,
A picture is worth 1000 words,

I am melody of shattered stained glass
A thousand times,
Mosaic of mystery and mayhem
Crumbling under the weight of my own
expectations—
All I know is rock and hard place,
Masquerade and face paint,
I been painting these smiles
From cheek to cheek
Untamed and wild like rivers flowing,
Though,
I still cannot tell the difference between
Real or fake,
Forgotten what I look like,
Been sweeping myself under the rug
Been searching in all the wrong places for love;
And realized—
I got a graveyard in my closet
No wonder my past continues to haunt me,
Lost religion;
Like an abandoned, humble tabernacle
Been searching for temple,
In this shack of a man,

Truth is,

I'm so close to broken,

So fragile,

Been agony,

Been defeat

Hoping to be every bit of masterpiece,
A living concerto called victory but
I'm still learning how to use this instrument
Fine tuning the ocean melody in my heartbeat
Find Jesus in me and walk across these rough seas—

But, all I know is heathen—   Faith?

What's faith when you do not believe in yourself?

       Self—

I don't believe in you.

Not sure who does anymore,
You used to be fire,
All you knew was flame
Always—
Now, you just smoke and ember
Fading to black like the end of
A tragic love story,
I see flaw, in your reflection,
Imperfect imperfections,
You stand, like a disappointing question
Unanswered,
Unstable on two legs and I—
I just need something to lean on
That doesn't resemble
Doubt or hesitation,

And holding this chin up isn't as easy as it looks,
Especially with a mouth heavy with uncertainty

Hoping to spew it out like luke-warm rhetoric

      Self—

I been concocting counterfeit confidence for you,
To mask,

      Your weak

      My blemish,

      This wrong

For too long;
This skin, has not felt like home
Guess I'm still mapping the unknown
Trying to Star Trek to the deep space of this lost souls galaxy

And BIG BANG!

Into my own,
And realize,
I am all hustle and heart,
All kinds of never quit
A hard-glowing fist full of grandmother's grace,
Every bit all father's son,
Mother's answered prayers,
Every bit of you
I used to be,
This 5-foot, 11' tsunami destined to crash into greatness
Leaving legacy in my aftermath, with a beautiful I love you
For a smile

      Self—

You are no fairy tale,
Far from happy ending or
Misplaced metaphor,
You are odyssey,

Labyrinth,
The way through,
You are lock and key
All work in progress,
You are growth
Are growing still,

Everything I hope to be
Everything I could never live without
Everything I love about me
Fruition of all my dreams,

     Self—

I need to be honest with you
So, I can start to

BELIEVE;

in me

WRITING

writing

is no chore;

it is

picking up all the broken

and

finally seeing

how

beautiful

i am

LETTING GO

Letting go;

Has become an involuntary reflex,

It is not that I'm cold—

My heart

Just…

Never been able to handle loss,

Too afraid of losing pieces of myself,

While,

Carrying a piece of anyone else

MIND/HEART

S o m e t i m e s;

I don't know where to begin,

MIND

Keeps interrupting my heart
fumbling over its words,

Saying,
"How can you lead, if you cannot direct his steps?"

HEART

Responds,
"To follow me is to follow a feeling, not take direction"

PROTECT

My heart—

Only knows to give

E V E R Y T H I N G;

Knows no fear,
Only love and abundance,

My mind—

Is all skeptic
Too hesitant and cautious,
Only knows to protect

MY H E A R T

ALL I HEAR

It's not that

I don't listen to my heart,

It's just sometimes,

When I do,

All I hear

Is the ocean

FIST

My H E A R T,

Is no lock

With some missing key,

It is a fist, clinched tight;

Wanting to feel safe enough to

...O P E N

STILL LEARNING

To be a man is to know—

It is okay to cry

I—

Am still learning

To be a man

MY SILENCE

My silence
Is restraint,
It is a choke hold on
My ego,
Male privilege,
And fragile masculinity—

                My silence
                Is a lesson
                In empathy,
                In listening,
                And in understanding—

                              My silence
                              Is necessary
                              For growth

MASCULINITY

On masculinity—

I will no longer claim you,
You are no good thing,

Only fragile,

Only broken

Only toxic

I will be a better man
Without you

I HAVE KNOWN

I have known pain;

      The kind that feasts on you slow,
      The kind that boa constricts
      Then swallows
      All your broken,
      Leads you away from light
      To the arms of depression

I have known healing;

      Remained whole
      Despite the feast,
      Became a self-love ballad
      Escaped the hold of depression

I have known survival

WHEN YOUR PEN GOES SILENT

when your pen goes silent—

inevitably, complacency sets in like
early onset Alzheimer's and you will
forget how to write revolutions-

your pen will feel like a clumsy
ballerina across page that forgot the
choreography, purpose will be but a
word you whisper to the pages of
your ever closed journal, 5 am will
feel like an awkward stranger nestled
next to you in bed, your
conversations with the moon will
seem crescent, or one sided, you will
feel like drought and desert and
fading sands in an hour glass

you will die a little each day, lose faith
in your gift, stop believing it was
meant for you, forget all that it has
meant to you— like, how my pen
saved my life, turned suicide notes
into reasons to live

these poems been flickering lantern
in my darkest days, been serenity and
sanctuary from the monsters under
my bed, been ocean rip tide to
drown my sin

when your pen goes silent—

you will think nothing of the upside
down, you've survived stranger
things, but depression will coil
around you, then swallow you slow
like an ancient basilisk; you will not
believe its depression, cause you do

not get depressed and we do not talk
about depression—

but you will realize, these poems been
therapy, prozac and zoloft and
vaporized ganja when i needed them
most, you will feel heavy and fragile,
broken in all the wrong places, waiting
to finally inhale deep; you will self-
diagnose, call it, writer's block, say I'm
waiting for inspiration, but you will
forget

what it feels like, what it looks like, how
it tastes, say; i need the right
environment, but will no longer
recognize the oasis you have always
been— home, won't feel like it, more
asylum, and white walls closing in, say, I
will write tomorrow but, it's always
tomorrow, excuses will mountain
around you until you are but a
mysterious crater and doubt; the fire
that was my eyes is barely glowing ash
and smoke;

when your pen goes silent—

your universe will collapse like a
desolate dwarf star until you are a black
hole in deep space and nothingness; you
will hide in your room under covers and
wish life was but a lucid dream I'd awake
from soon, how you will swell with
tears cause writing is the only way I
know how to cry, the only way I know
how to feel, the only way I know how
to pray, and breathe deep; writing,
proof my pen has been sword of
protection and omens, fending off this
doom, this darkness these demons of
depression—

so, when my pen goes silent; it's like
sheathing a sword in the midst of
fighting a dragon, depression is a
dementor's kiss, stealing my happiness
and gnawing at my smile; it is no
creature of myth, it is the space
between rock and hard place, as tangible
as silence and forever, it be taboo,
unjustified stigma, societal shame and
medication,

it is crying wolf and no one coming until
you are aftermath, it is a debilitating
noose, keeping pen and pad just out of
reach;

until everything is—

silent

SHARDS

I am shards of shattered stained glass being pieced together daily—

Usually, when rendezvousing with midnight or when the light of morning cracks darkness in half; an impossible jigsaw of man cocooning too frequent to recognize who I once was.

Change; has made me all unfamiliar reflection, growth has made me all stretch mark uncomfortable, silence is all cliché these days; deafening and loud.

I am an argument and mantra
Prayer and meditation,
Conflict and choreography beautiful.

My past, an elaborate unforgettable scar, too jagged edged and more meaningful than I probably realize, my heart a weary survivor still beating little drummer boy symphony hoping to be strong enough to love again—

I am still just a student, and life, a professor, teaching as if I should already know the answers and testing on what was never taught;

My purpose, this faint echo that I cannot quite make out, has haunted me too long; it lingers in corners, falls between cracks, and gets lost in translation.

How I have made too many excuses thus far; mistakes, I have misrepresented as short comings. Still navigating through the galaxy in my eyes and the truth in the mirror, still making a way against a violent rip tide of pride, a constant commanding current causing conflict and confusion.

I feel nothing, just the strain of muscle and mind over all that never mattered. Hope; doesn't live here anymore, in this broken home under destruction. Trying to be all progress, in process, but I am still at war with insecurity and sometimes my tongue turns traitor, all tortuous and talon. How it makes this temple feel like ruin. How I still haven't learned to cry, or empathize, or even allow sympathy to find me. How I hide in plain sight like a reanimated mannequin learning to do something other than smile.

Too often I find doubt in my stars and questions in my throat, uncertainty in my voice and the audacity in my tone won't seem to hang on to every word. And I am still, mostly writing poems about myself these days, holistic remedies, I recite daily like morning prayers, sustenance for my spirit that only knows, hunger.

STILLNESS

There is so much stillness—

And,
I am all aftermath searching for survival,
My smile,
Still the best defense mechanism I own

I am all depleted arsenal these days—
Calm and reflective,

How my mind relapses with the past,
How I drift,
A lazy river of memories and what if

And I swore—

I would never live this way
But I can't help but to hoard all that I let go

All that I know has happened
And this present is so unstable,

My future—
All dream and expectation,

And,
I hope, the weight of it all,
Has made me strong enough to see, it through

FIRE

It has been said,

I am all fire,
A smoldering flame
Emitting too much heat to know closeness,
Unwilling to be extinguished
And,
Too mesmerized by my own glow.

I say,

Sometimes,

Heat be necessary for my own protection,
Why douse my flame for your comfort?
And, yes—
It took a long time to find beauty in my glow
So,
I must be tinder

to myself

ONCE

I,

      Was once a river,

Spanning   across   foreign   lands

Without rapids,

      Just slow bends
      and winding turns

                    Collecting memories like sediment

My heart believes,

                          I am still a river

ROAD TRIP

The way to my heart;

    is a road trip

                                            with good music,

                        amazing food,

and the constant fear

                              of running out of gas...

TO LOVE ME

to love me

is to know,

F
   R
        U
           S
              T   R   A
                            T
                                I
                                  O
                                    N

LOVE LANGUAGE

Love—

Is no word;

It   is,   an   entire   language.

INTRIGUE

I told her,

The
    curves
        of
     your
body

don't interest me—

but,

The beauty of your mind,

Renders

Unrelenting

Intrigue

DOWN THE SLIDE

I was 8, and

A Curious George of a boy

Had already learned girls were nectar

And sweet—

Knew, if I turned them smile and giggle

Agave would seep from their lips,

And I—

Couldn't wait to taste,

Made my first promise

I never intended to keep,

Grabbed her by the hand

Unleashed a smile

Turning me

Georgie Porgie Pudding Pie

And then, I kissed her,

Going down the slide

KISS ME

Kiss me

           with all the fervor

      of our first,

                  with all your soul

           as if it be our last

Kiss me

        daily

     like this

          or,

                    don't kiss me at all

CLING

CLING—

    to me,

        like

need is all you know;

    And I—

        am   EVERYTHING

SIMULTANEOUSLY

to love—

is to let go
and,
to hold on

simultaneously

A LOVER LIES

When you learn;
A lover told a lie—
It will feel like a lesson in, how to get away with murder,
It will haunt you,

Keep you all insomniac reliving the past,
Sleep, won't feel the same for a while and
Neither will your bed, but
The ceiling and your eyes will love affair until you find answers,

How time flies when you are lost,
Wandering through a tainted forest of memories
You now want to burn,
Randomly;

Your teeth will clench,
Hate will boil up and steam through your eyes
Tears Niagara
How you will regret ever falling

Deep diving into what you believed to be
Crystal blue ocean deep—
Now you wonder,
How much swamp did you navigate through?

There will be no pain
Instead,
You will be all Novocain and numb
Cold to the tone in your voice,

Emotions all frigid and frost bite,
The indifference in your smile will shadow any facade you attempt,
You will find solace in silence—
Those moments you forget everything

But beware,
Reminders are everywhere
Like, your bed and the ceiling
How they have become all Harvey Dent now

Remember,
When your ceiling was the place to go to get lost in a daydream
And,
Your bed

Once laced with your lover's scent
Now–
It is residue you cannot wash away

Slowly,
As time passes,
You will acquire mechanisms of defense
Learning to block what happened,
Until—

You are blindsided by,
A text,
Or a picture
How it turns you all inside out with question and riddle

Like—
If you missed me,
Then,
Why did you lie an underground railroad to escape what we had?

Or
If a picture is worth 1000 words,
Then how many of those words are truths
And, how many were lies?

How you will wish you paid closer attention in statistics class.
How you will feel sick to your stomach,
How letting go feels so easy right now,
How the numbness subsides,
How the forest burns,
How the shine of your smile finally leaves no place for shadow,

Forgiveness—
Will come like a reluctant super-hero to save you from yourself
When you learn, a lover told a lie
It will eat at everything you were,
Until—

You are everything you are now

BLACK WOMAN

They say—
I don't have eyes for you.

Tell me,
I don't understand the power that
lies in your breath,
Or the forever in your tone,

They say—
I fear your strength,
As if I be too coward to explore the
nebula in your eyes;

They say—
I am blind to your majesty,
As if, queen is all you be

They say—
You too much resilience
Too much fight song, negro spiritual
And heart for me to conquer;
Like you could ever be conquered—
Dressed in every bit of overcome
and defiance
Winged fearless
How I orbit the world that lie in your
hips,
Respect the rhythm and rock steady
in your walk

They say—
I am blind to your beauty,

As if, your beauty ain't archetype to
beautiful
And, your natural all captivating
catalyst for righteous rebellion

You,
More mimicked matriarch of style,
Master of moon and motherhood,

I love you

Have since, I laid eyes on my mother
Witnessed grandmother carry a
family in the midst of Alabama hate
and racism
Emerged all bounty and business
woman wonderful,
How can I not have eyes for you,
black woman!

I see you
You, glorious gladiator of grace
Over-worked and under praised
phenomenal woman,
Ingenious,
Innovator of ingenuity,
Way maker from no way,
Rock and strong hold of pride and
perseverance,
Never silent soulful sapient
Struggle and elegance;
You rise, inevitable
Like a phoenix from ash and flame
Overflowing forgiveness and faith
You—
A bare-knuckle Molotov cocktail of a
woman,
But; I fear for you,

Because they fear your defiance,
Too eager to turn you ghost and disappearing act
And my mouth all obituary and remembrance
How they refuse to speak your name like they know,
Not to take it in vain,
You, God, Earth, Mother, woman
A hallelujah anyhow,
A universe fighting to survive in a society
That finds faults in your stars
In your darkness,
The vastness of your shape,
Formed for a struggle the world will never understand—

The hardest thing to be is,

A black woman—
But; you carry the weight of black and woman like a scepter
Conjuring black girl magic
With your smile, your side eye, your confidence,
Your love, a full and abundant harvest

How black man, would not be black man without you,
Just black boy attempting to rise,
Forever, bending but never breaking backbone of family,
How you stand courageous
Even when black man is turned into chalk outline
And media makes mockery of his character,

How this black man, could never be
black man without you

So, when they say,
I don't have eyes for you,
Maybe they are right—
Cause I have so much more,

I have this voice for you,
This smile,
My love for you
This heart,
I have my forever for you
And, maybe
If I be so lucky,
A black woman will turn me all
humble bended knee
And I will present a dowry of my
heart and soul
For an eternity shared with you

MEMORY

Initially,
I didn't think this necessary, but the thought
of you has lingered, old and stale, reeking of
past mistakes; your voice, crowds the
empty hallways of what was once a place
we called our own, you— are more
remembered than forgotten these days

Remember,
When we met— Our eyes played tag all
night, you wore an invitation for a smile— I,
I perpetrated oblivious and disinterest
though I was covered in curiosity and
intrigue, approached you, like I write
poems, deliberate and purposeful; reduced
your wall to rubble, spun hesitation to
eager willingness, you wrote your number
on receipt paper, which I kept until not too
long ago

Remember,
When we kissed— The night before the
morning I left, it was pure cocaine, or how I
would imagine it, I was nothing less than
too far gone

Remember,
It feels like a million moons ago, I left
thinking you— Nothing more than this
explosive fling, I was so wrong, our
inception, knocked me off axis; we kin to
late nights, connecting hearts, tracing stars
in the sky with conversation, you explored
my depths, you ransacked the corners of
my mind, I had never been so transparent—
naked

Remember,

When we made love, we were communion,
all body and praise, idle worship and sin, we
ascension and revelation, reaching zenith
together, it was all too good to be true—
Told you, I love you, didn't know what else
it could be, if not love then what; made
Facebook a witness, I had never done that
before; how I was all free fall and hope back
then

Then,
June came, like white smoke and the crack
of tinder before a blaze, thought we could
turn a house into a home and us into
happily ever after, but all that happened was
me learning, to Rubik's cube myself to make
you happy, and all you did was find more
and more distance to put between us, I
never felt so far away, but we always had
communion, getting drunk on the wine
before we devoured the body, it's the only
thing we were good at

Remember,
For a year, we played house pretending to
be happy and in love— the end came, like a
slow suicide with no note; how we slit
wrists with silence, held secrets closer than
we held each other, didn't understand how
I was suffocating in an empty house, our
relationship was all noose around my neck,
and I hung on your every word and
possibility, how foolish was I then

Remember,
When this house of cards collapsed, you all
tears and smeared make up, I was
unconcerned and cold, never thought I'd be
recovery and detox, but remember;

Remember,

How we relapsed, reuniting with night, like
two junkies who scraped up enough change
for a hit, it's like we couldn't not get high
on each other, turning our place all dope
house and waterfalls; but even the addiction
let go, it was the last thing we lost in the
fire, finally we abandoned the ember, the
flames and ash— I haven't seen or heard
from you, I think you're married now, I
hope happy, I found refuge in poems

Remember,
When you pushed me to perform for the
first time, you should see what I built, how
paramount are you; not sure you'd
recognize me now, or I you, but I thank
you; you introduced me to the suffering
past the pain, because of you, I learned to
push through and make it past the pain, I
haven't found love since, but I found myself,
and I promise to never lose that again

SHEETS OF MUSIC

In silence,

Solitude and darkness

    I fantasize—

How we turn origami,
Howling at new moons,
Reading bodies in braille
Rhythm and blues our breath

We
Holy, heathen, harmony, and hope
Nothing more than understanding, here—
Spoken in tongues,
Deep, soothing, elongated syllables
Echoing

We
Freedom of expression
Chronicle of past stars
Refraction of dawns early light,

Wanting—

Wades in the water of our tide

Patience;

A prescribed aphrodisiac

Reality—

Runs wild until it is imagination again

Bliss;

Runneth over in waves

We

Baptized in endless possibilities
but there is no love here—
Just ravenous exploration

We
Nothing more than exquisite sheets of music

Still—
Waiting for someone to discover our song

AMUSEMENT PARK

Told me—

I was just an amusement park

And she—

Was only here for the attraction

And,

All   rides

the

BROKEN PROMISE

We kissed like a broken promise, an unfaithful conspiracy, there was no place for innocence, there were only seductive intentions, no hesitation; guilt and disappointment waited for us on the other side of the threshold; lustful deceit fueled this passion, eyes closed tight, so there were no witnesses to indiscretion, in darkness we disturbed silence, it was no longer welcome; romantic it was not, primal maybe; we stripped away all hope, fear and doubt; revealing our true selves to each other offering flesh as we sacrificed life as we knew it

Exposed hidden desires, carnal hunger and irresistible longing, we acted on instinct, obviously reliving a fantasy that had played on an infinite loop in our minds; we would not taint this moment with impending consequence, there would be no regret, no wanting, no stone unturned, no desire unfulfilled, there would be only satisfaction, fulfillment, indulgence; we lost our selves in possibility, an imperfect arrangement of an intimate orchestration; we were rhapsody in blue, 5th symphony, we were 9th Wonder instrumental, once sampled, we mixed and it took no time to master this production, We— engineered for this moment, our sound tracked ceiling corners, then returned as a whisper…

Take me—

All the permission I needed, proceeded to kiss her breath away, tasted every inch of flesh, hands explored her wonderland, over mounds, through valleys, across great plains, hoping to stake claim to this new world, read her goose bumps like an open invitation in braille; she was an open book of secrets, spoke them like gospel, in tongues, she moaned hymnals in praise, to all that might be; she tree of knowledge, everything good and evil I never knew; so I savored her forbidden fruit, until she runneth over, on this bed of betrayal, my rod and staff comfort her, she embraced, caressed my ego, partook in my manhood like she was trying to teach a new language, then slowly

I entered her Eden, plunged every inch of integrity I had left into her, watched her exhale righteousness, and I lost all virtue in those sheets, but our lips, our lips came together like a lightning strike to earth, 500 million volts of life locked my arms around her and her nails into me, we became one, a beast with two backs, a slow spinning tornado, wrapped in infidelity, no forever on the horizon, just a one night, understanding, from bed to floor, from floor to wall, we tattooed this moment in rapture, our bodies, entangled in ecstasy, a twisted temptation; we contorted into positions that changed like we were trying to sample them all, repeatedly submerged then surfaced attempting to explore new depths, until I felt her body shake, we weren't making love, we earth quaked, came together like tectonic plates, causing tsunamis, and seismic explosive eruptions we were an unpredictable unnatural disaster, fantasy and nightmare, pleasure and sorrow, we were aftermath and destruction, a beaming light of transgression

We; were sorry, sweaty, and gasping for air— stared at the ceiling, thankful these walls, couldn't talk; we gathered our breath and collected the courage to say, something— but silence returned, so we kissed, again, this time like late night conversation, turned argument that neither one of us wanted to lose

We were an unfaithful conspiracy,

Another broken promise

ALL THAT MATTERS

My heart beats slow, 32 degrees below zero, a tundra soul, vast as solar systems and unknown; like far away stars and distant galaxies, to say this man is a simple creature is fallacy— slowly, gradually, growing, tired of feeling the stares of sexy silent silhouettes of seductive eyes attempting to obtain attention, if only briefly, tired of tasting forbidden fruit under cloak of night, but never really feeling full of anything, but myself, tired of late nights and early mornings, tired of my ceiling fan being the only one to whisper sweet nothings, feeling nothing, but maybe,

just maybe, I want to find love true, but not sure I can anymore, not sure I can see past intentions, or women's disguises, or traps set, then hidden between thighs, I hear the plagues in their lies, trying to infect me with versions of the truth, and she thinks, she can wield womanly ways, whisper wishes, with the wonder of her unknown, but I've known that power since age 12,

truth is, she, hoping to venture bed chambers, disrobe loins, exploit body, under covers, and climax, before she even reaches my pinnacle, but doesn't know pleasure will never conquer my mind, truth is she, not ready to quest for my heart, to journey to forever, too fearful of falling too hard, I've learned, under stars that not everything in dark comes to light, and sometimes, you have to come to darkness and see for yourself, sometimes

I fall in lust on purpose, 'cause I know it's temporary, a phase, and I know my heart is safe, combination is PI and they ask why my name is (e)nfinite, it's so simple to me but, not so simple to see, but they rarely even try... Too concerned with matters of the flesh, but that's only skin deep, though I'll admit, I've looked into the eyes of seduction, and smiled, been intoxicated off passion, devoured fantasies and licked my lips after tasting sin, in the heat of late nights I branded satisfaction all over anatomies, left bodies in breathless bliss gasping for more and I even cuddled insecurities

and I bet, I bet they thought they could handle it, so they wagered desires for the jackpot, of my love, but crapped out, cause I never gamble with my emotions, hell, I'm still collecting pieces of my shattered heart, bread crumbs, to know where I've been, not sure I'll ever go back so, I'll just be patiently waiting for the one, my better half, a star crossed lover, a once labeled heart breaker, because how can you reassemble what you've never taken apart, when it comes to matters of the heart, I don't completely understand, possibly I'm just too common, the dreamer, the believer, cause I've been dreaming of the woman I told my mother about years ago and still believing she actually exists

I know, I'm too old to still believe in fairy tales, but that's just the hopeless romantic in me, my mother warned me of days like this, told me patience is a virtue, but too often temptation is often too tempting to resist, and pleasure too pleasing to the palate to be patient, and I just want to breathe, no take my breath away, take my mind to the clouds, let's kiss the sky, let's get high on intelligent conversation, let's lay it all on the table; your secrets, my skeletons, your doubts, my hesitation, our hopes, our dreams, let's build a love with all we have left, nothing more or less,

Let's stop playing all the fucking games—

I've never been good at charades; I understand, your heart's been broken, mine too, but I think hearts were meant to be broken, to be shattered, to be missing pieces; how else are you supposed to find the one who completes you; how else do you become whole; how else do you reassemble if you've never had one broken apart, finally, I'm starting to understand

All that matters, is the heart

ALTERING SKYLINES

She—

Is a mountain of a woman

But too often;

Her beauty falls on the eyes of adventurers

Who only envision conquest;

Their eyes feasting on her terrain

Coveting her pinnacle

Blinded, hoping to lay claim

How they miss her majesty—

Taking for granted her ability to alter skylines

Forgetting, the sun rises from her shoulders,

and the moon falls into her chest

MAGIC

She—

Was all forward and charming
confidence;

Forced herself into my days like
an overzealous sunrise, I saw
every bit of moon in her eyes,
her smile held future like it was
the only possibility, I, all earth and
boulder and she; was sky— my
only hope to share an infinite kiss,
to meet at the horizon,
remarkably, she made that
impossibility feel so tangible; so
real, how swiftly I was drawn in
to her, like a good book of
poems, she was my favorite and I
hers, we read together, nightly,
recited her like a mantra,
hummed her like an old hymn;

Our genesis, written in laughs, in
smiles, across midnights and so
many miles, scribbled notes in her
margin; bookmarked my favorite
pages in silence; we had these
moments, that said everything
even when we said nothing I felt
so, kid again, you know, back
when truly believed in magic;
before you learned it's a trick, all
smoke and mirror deception

Told me,

My willingness to be vulnerability,
was my best trait, honesty, all I
ever needed, so I offered,

acceptance, because it's the key to everyone's heart,

Told me,

She deserved me, because she was good woman,

Told her,

I deserved her because I couldn't wait to be a good man, the one my mother raised, I've just been needing a reason—

Believed, she was all the oxygen this fierce flame would ever need, but realized, she was merely bated breath on the smoldering embers of my heart, just enough to stir me to a warm glow of pride and compliment; took my smile beyond infinity, birthed hope, killed the sinister skeptic I've always been, my heart was all butterfly and orchid bloom after storm, I heard it said, faith be no easy task, but she was all proof and evidence of happily ever after

So, she will never be regret, or bad decision—

Though she be Siren— all myth and tall tale betrayal, just another trick masquerading as magic, how she dragon balled after I wished for her, said she had to return to her past, to rewrite its future, left me wanting, longing for a forever that was merely fairytale, there was once symphony and sunrise but now there's only silence and dusk before dawn, how quickly we lose faith, how quickly forever turns to timeline of memory, you could never forget, how genesis became revelation, funny it's always true believers who tarnish a good book

Said, she had grown tired of losing pieces, so she spent her nights between two kings in hopes of a castle, crossing borders, possibility was but a pawn she sacrificed at my feet to prove loyalty, but I was the one she advanced on, but never the one she retreated to so I should have known, we weren't on the side.

She broke my heart—

Left the pieces in a long text message I couldn't bring myself to reply to, that truth harder to swallow than a hand full of broken glass, I wonder if she knew how I had to claw my heart from my chest to give, chewing through doubt, hesitation, gut feeling, or how I unshackled my emotions with a key I hid under my skin, there is scar now, was once a gaping wound where all my hope bled through, never learned first aid, never learned to stopped the bleeding, just to let it flow thick

It only takes the body a few days to replenish lost blood, only a few smiles to give me hope again, only acceptance to stop the bleeding, I am ocean, all ebb and flow, current and tidal wave, my chest, is no tomb of brick and mortar to protect my heart from thieves, I am only a man, a good man still waiting for a woman, a good woman

That makes me believe in magic

DATING SUCKS

i know nothing

>of diamonds,
>of shine,
>of eternity or
>of forever—

i know nothing

>of bended knee,
>of submission or
>of praise

i know nothing

>of falling,
>of lips,
>of hands,
>of touch or
>of love.

but i do know, that

DATING FUCKING SUCKS!

and ain't nobody got time for that, bullshit,
i have been single for:

4 years,
6 months,
1 week,
10 days,
12 hours
21 minutes
and 17 seconds,

dating is a chore,
no— a job,
matter of fact;
it's internship

because it just hasn't paid off,

phone calls,
now all text messages
and learning to read between the lines,

and dates, are meet up groups

and intimacy is now synonymous with sex,

now i know,

there are plenty of fish in the sea,
but i want chemistry that sparks,
but i can't find a match,
can't seem to maintain a flame
without a bit of tinder,
and my heart is up here,
not down there, OK Cupid,

i remember,
when it was all so easy,
before dating became online shopping,
no courtship;
back when, interpersonal relationships
were actually, interpersonal
and not via social media or online

and, it's all a game—
i've been playing Russian roulette
hoping to be blown away,
but there's no bullets in this gun,
i've been walking this cliff's edge
and my family just wants me to fall,
but there's something to be said of balance,
i've been trying to Jacques Cousteau
the depths of women i meet
but not in the way they want me to,

I've been trying and failing,
trying and failing

just, trying to date,

you know meet,
curious eyes and smiles first,
all compliment and introduction,
watch each other butterfly through conversation,
hearts flutter a clumsy waltz of possibility,
exchanging numbers like secret combinations,
how first call,
feels all plummeting rollercoaster, and free-
how first date makes you wish it will never end,
how lips bloom for first kiss,
how lips feel like you've never been kissed after,
how kiss feels like first hit,
how addiction sets in;
how infatuation makes you forget, to learn more,
how sex ruins everything;
but makes everything better,
how compromise makes you ask how we got here;
looking in the mirror makes you question what you see

i don't know what this is;
and no, I don't know where we are going,
i just know

i don't want this anymore—

i know nothing

    of dating,
    of relationships, or
    of how to make things work

But i know everything

    of collapse,
    of dismantled,
    of destruction,
    of rubble and aftermaths,
    of apocalypse,

and how to leave wanting and needy grieving

for everything I never promised,

dating has become a practice
in making nothing into something,
then calling it what it's always been,

it's become a hobby
i can't seem to get better at,

it's a tug of war between substance and lust
and lust always wins,
hell, substance as hasn't picked up the rope in a while,

dating, is a game of truth or dare,
we, all daring with our bodies,
because we, too afraid to tell truth with our mouths,

it has made me realize when i say,
it's not you it's me,
it's the truest thing I've said to myself in a long time,
too often I end up with the wrong women,

who will know nothing

    of a forever,
    of praise,
    of falling, or
    of my heart but
    of everything

on how not to do it like this again
and i can't seem to learn that lesson

i know nothing

    of diamonds,
    of bended knee,

i know nothing

    of Love

i just know

dating fucking sucks

SNEAKERHEAD

I'm a sneaker head

A kicks lover

Some say,

Sneaker-holic but

I prefer, sole searcher—
In search of rare, on the
prowl for pristine, the
kicks of my dreams,
I'm so serious right now,

What you know about this
kick game?

You can catch me stomping
in my Air Force Ones, or
so fresh and so clean,
clean in my Dunk SB's;
and I got Air Max on max
on max and my Adidas,
are my first love, Shell-
toes, Gazelle, Somoas,
Campus's— I pay homage
to Chuck Taylor, but I
just never convert to
converse

What you know about
Tinker Hatfield? What
you know about them J's?
My favorite's got to be
Bred 11's, Concords,
Space Jams, Mars 4's,
Grape 5's, can't forget
the Cement 3's, I love

retros but prefer the OG's, please believe; my kick game is sick, somebody better call a doctor, I promise, you ain't got these, probably wouldn't know where to find them, I guess, I have to remind them

This ain't a hobby, it's a lifestyle, more like a declaration to my style, cause you don't know about those quick strike color ways or hyper strike J's, laser etched designs by Mark Smith, or a pair of Sabotage kicks, I ain't gassing you up but my kicks stay premium, just like those Levi x Nike Dunk collabos', Supreme NYC's, man I got to have those, and I'm cleaning out my closet, just to make room for some Yeezy's or some Galaxy Foamposites, and I stay online searching and researching new releases

I JUST LOVE NEW SNEAKERS!

You don't know about this kick game! It's an addiction, 'cause you can get in too deep, 'cause it's like every week I need a fix, guess you can call me a fiend for kicks, 'cause when I get that itch; I gotta cop, gotta score more footwork, and my limited funds, fund my elaborate endeavors, as I hit the local skate shop on payday, wishing the Nike outlet had layaway, Foot Locker helped pave the way for this obsession, I'm a Champ, so I run into the Finish Line where it all started and I used to Journey to the Underground Station with Jimmy Jazz until I met up with Dr Jay, but my favorite gotta be hitting up those unique sneaker boutiques, I Wish, I could cop kicks every day

To me, this kick game, isn't a game at all it's a part of me, my culture, as I display pieces of my personality, a perfected protest to perception, a portrayal of my past, present and future,

So, why this kick game all fucked up!

I'm tired of the killings over limited editions at major retailers, sick of the ebay, Instagram, and Facebook resellers; disappointed in fraudulent websites selling counterfeits as originals and consignment store prices are criminal. I guess, I'm just a cog in this machine. A pawn and kicks are king.

But what you know about this kick game?

You know,

Nike, has 54% of the US shoe market on lock a perpetually rising stock, but their factories abroad still being accused of being sweat shops, workers over worked, humiliated, under paid, no minimum wage, mandatory overtime, no overtime pay, exploiting child labor in countries where child labor has no rules or laws, and they do little things like complaining and they lose their job, using cheaper labor, the cheapest material, but continually raising prices, economically amputating a people; to a sneaker head like me, a sneaker is

becoming more and
more like a blood
diamond.

But I'm still—in search of
rare, on the prowl for
pristine, the kicks of my
dreams, but I never knew
my collection stems from
so much oppression, I
look in the mirror and
question.

I'm sneaker head?

I'm a kicks lover?

Wait,

What you really know about this kick game?

MY BLACK SKIN

It be a miracle;
A testament to survival,
An ode in the key of,
We still here!

Ain't it precious?

Ain't it a dilemma?

What it mean to be loved and hated,
Envied and feared,
Hunted—

Ain't it strong as fuck;

It be no burden
Weighing on my shoulders
But—
A celebration carried in my smile

Ain't it precious

YOU UNRULY BEAST

You strange case of Dr Jekyll and Mr. Hyde, you; unlikely smile, you frustrating daily reminder, a virtuous vision of virility, you are manly as shit— sexy as hell, a silent conversation creator, my partner in crime I, salute you

My beard, celebrated nappy fleeced frame of my smile, who knew your reluctant genesis would spark an improbable odyssey, my face, just hasn't been the same, so beautifully unfamiliar, meticulously unkempt, incredibly fickle

We have been through thick and thin; and thick and thin again; but the constant, is growth, we've grown together, defiantly in arms, you've become both weakness and strength,

I, must be more Samson than I know, hell I've never been able to deny a Delilah either, my beard be rock ballad meets hip hop symphony, a righteous EDM rave of my soul, a slow building super hero anthem of first impression,

I could never imagine life without you, my parents, think you both bristly and bothersome more beast of burden, barely acceptable, wish, I would master the art of shaving, and retire you to stubble; but NEVER! Ok, maybe not never, but no time soon,

I've relearned commitment, dedication, learn to care for you; Team Natural!! And they be like, what kind of chemicals you got in there, and I be like, I put no chemicals, only juices and berries, beard oils, creams, balms and conditioners, I'm a bit obsessed, but you, yes you, are testimonial of resilience, symbol of self-love, wonder of my world, My beard, legendary; a poem my body is growing for me, man, my beard be like HUH! I woke up like this, I'm a boss, and hell, any man can start a beard but it takes a real man to finish one

Just know, I'm more militant now than last shave, shaggy beyond belief, but I can't seem to trim you, just can't seem to let go, so just grow, wild, and as uncivilized as they assume I am, grow dangerous like night, like Arizona Tea and Skittles, like fear's grown from follicles, be reason, they say

black, not reason, cause race,
not issue, my beard be issue
like warning shots into
ceilings; it stands its ground,
and grows brilliant, be shine I
shine, my beard, be mane

My beard a black fist in air, a
black power salute, peaceful
protest to status quo, and
they say it's unprofessional,
but we professionals 'cause
we broke the mold,

Though, I wish; I wish it was
defense to chokeholds, or
bulletproof, cause my skin be
target, yes bullseye, like black
skin begat killed by police, and
killed by police equals no
indictment, I guess my beard
be assumption of guilt, be
criminal, be violence, No!

My beard isn't just riots, it's
rooted in recollection from
which I came, it is belief in,
and a dare to dream, it is
freedom, remembrance of the
fallen and the rage against the
machine, there's untelevised
revolution hanging from this
chin, though, all they see is
stereotypes in my skin,

My beard— is strange fruit,
reminder that I could die too
soon, each strand of gray, a
memory of a time I survived
something that might have
killed me, my beard a flawless

unwavering hope that change,
is just one clean shave away

BACK IN THE DAY

Back in the day,
when I was young I'm not a kid anymore
but some days I sit and wish I was a kid again

Back in the day,
when I was young I'm not a kid anymore

I was Lego building,
Tree climbing,
Everything dismantling,
Back talking,
Big wheel riding,
Rock throwing,
Velcro shoe wearing,
Wheelie Popping,
Thunder Cats,
GI Joe,
Voltron,
Transformers, and
Silver Hawks watching,
Too many damn questions asking,
Mischievous, bad ass, hard headed little boy.

Forever—
At full speed with a gale force smile,
a lit bottle rocket,
waiting to fly and turn the sky into a jungle gym,
to play hide and seek in the clouds;
what other dreams does a boy have but these,
to be but a flailing wish amongst the stars,
to be a barefoot summer year round
with blackberry stained finger tips,
scraped knees, and elbows
in search of adventure and
secret hiding places and
unattended water hoses;
only concerned with the equitable distribution of ice cream,
the moment street lights turn a glow,
and the opinions of pretty pony tailed girls
double-dutching in the streets.

We—
were a legion of laughter and light,
back when I knew my friends by name,
not by color;
knew their phone numbers by heart,
knew my black only as beautiful,
knew love, only as innocent and
had not yet learned of loss
my heart, was not yet a lock that needed a key,
and my joy was endless,
my joy was simple,
it came in the morning
it's amazing, I didn't have much
but I never felt without,
the only fear I had,
was not being able to go outside
and fling myself into a breeze,
with no regard for my body, but

My body—
has always been something
my parents weren't sure was going to make it home
I have always known the worry in mother's voice,
the concern, in my father's tone,
every time they called my name,
meaning, they knew, one day I may not answer!
I wonder if my parents ever believed me safe
ever fell asleep, unafraid for my life.

As a kid—my parents
always told me to be beware of strangers,
and be back before dark,
like they knew strangers and
the darkness were the only things that could take me,
and now, every time we get off the phone,
they tell me to be safe out there and take care,
and I know that means, beware;
they will come for you too,
they are turning black bodies to ghosts,
and we do not want to lose you
and these days,

I can't tell you the last time
I fell asleep not thinking of my own death
wondering if a bullet, would finally be
my ticket to the clouds,
making me a flailing wish amongst the stars,
a black body staining the streets.

And I miss; I miss when my heart beat was a joyous noise
and my only fear was messing up my good clothes,
now my heart is a somber hymn of remembrance
and the fear of death is constantly with me,
my smile used to be an endless exuberant praise,
and my eyes were full of rejoice and light and
I felt safe, but now being hyper-vigilant is
weighing me down every day and
every night has become a practice in gratefulness,
because I didn't die,
every morning if not filled with mourning,
is a constant search for my joy,
and all I can think is,

I remember way back when,
I remember way back when,

Back in the day, when I was young I'm not a kid anymore but some days

I sit and wish

I was a kid again

COLOR BLIND

Our eyes met, like rushing pedestrians on a crosswalk going the opposite direction who bumped shoulders

The jolt; turned everything cinematic slow-motion, my eyes wandered her silhouette searching for a reason to speak, though nothing clever came to mind, her smile was an unexpected star in a lonely sky.

Our conversation, started and stumbled over miraculous coincidences pausing only for laughter, we; flirtatious, excited, and nervous, parted ways with curiosity seeds in our pockets, a hope to fertilize their growth, and a 10-digit combination that could unlock an unlikely future

Admittedly, I was inspired by the mystery and intrigue of it all, our phone calls traversed sunsets and sunrises without stopping to refuel, we slowly undressed our truths; her voice was the perfect piano to accompanying the bass in my heart, she seemed all delicate bird of paradise portrait in 10,000 pieces,

nothing less than a beautiful time bomb with an hour glass frame

One day I asked,

"Have you ever dated a Black man?"

Her reply, was the tragic collapse of everything we built, I don't see color, fell guillotine swift from her lips, I became all fist and survival mode, blood rioting through my veins, explained, if you don't see color then you can't see me, this skin is nothing to turn a blind eye to, heavy with burden, with history and the responsibility of too many to name.

You will not diminish who I am to seem accepting, or to make us more palatable; this blackness, be nothing you can ever deny, nothing that can ever be unseen, it be my greatest gift, they say, it be my only curse.

To be color blind is no cure for racism, only a way to white wash my identity, and lived experiences, a cute attempt to sweep the problem of racial inequality under the rug, as if racial prejudice vanishes because you refuse to see it, to see this black be no taboo, though it carries the stigma of a society who continues to deny the problem, systemic racism is no figment of the imagination, it be a plague in a nation that claims to be indivisible.

I ask,

"Do you not see the racial inequity?"

White mass murderer, arrested, unarmed black man killed by police officer who receives administrative leave; white kid shoots up a church, arrested, unarmed black teen gunned down by police with no indictment to follow.

This skin be feared, it be probable cause, guilty, be prosecuted at higher rates, sentenced to longer terms; if only lady justice actually be as blind as you claim to be!

A deep breath ensues, the silence, heavy and thick like the humidity be in the South;

my heart a hyper metronome as the hope
we once were fades away

NEVER DIED

I knocked on the door,
Dressed; in my best "acceptable negro",
A tired empty smile stamped on my face,
Spouted my credentials like a reassurance of safety;
See, comfort and rapport are important in my line of work—

He looked, every bit of broken and hesitant,
lost then found,
But I've been known to look past warning signs,
Throw caution to the wind,
Invited, I entered his home;
It looked all,
How to become a hoarder, Volume 1,

His fear manifested in the form
of a small, 9mm pistol he revealed like a magic trick,

Saying,

    "you never know who may appear at your front door",

Flinching or sudden movements
were no longer an option,
I thought twice but arrogance
was all devil's advocate on my shoulder
advising me to stay, but

I was face to face with the devil,
Dressed, in his best racist white man—
We sat in his living room,
Me on the couch, him,
On a recliner he swiveled towards me,

My smile, a little less believable,
Covered my face like lousy graffiti,
Our conversation must have felt like,
Slave revolt, because his fear reappeared,
He showed me its dark throat and full belly,

I bet it couldn't wait to projectile vomit my life to memory;

He clutched his gun like
He was holding on to the last seconds of his life,
His demeanor morphed from reluctant host to vicious snake

And I, was still;
Not thinking of survival but of my mother
And it's been a while since I told her,
I love you,
Wondering who'd mourn me,
Turn me all hashtag, and media frenzy.
Who'd tell my truth?
I hope—

They make my body a peace offering,
An open casket sacrifice to America,
If I can be the last I will die here,
Invite a bullet to be laid to rest in my chest,
Let it ping pong in this body until they call the shot fatal.

They say, when you are face to face with death,
Your life flashes before your eyes,
There was no flash,
Just quiet and barely enough sun to sneak through the blinds;
He hoped for fear and panic,
they were nowhere to be found

Escape came slow, like
The equality we are still fighting for

He asked,

    "Are we finished"

I nodded yes, and
Rose like Jesus on the 3rd day
Eyes fixed on his trigger finger,
I backed away, felt my way to the hall,
Turned, reached for the front door,

He said,

    "Have a nice day", then

Smiled almost to revel in the moment,

I wanted to ask, is my skin your phobia?
Is it overwhelming threat?
Is it too loud and demanding of its own space?
Is it potential trophy or am I just another bullseye you have yet to hit?
Will you speak of this moment as accomplishment?
Is my existence only malleable in the mouths of white men with a
God complex and a pistol?

The sun greeted me like an old friend,
I eluded the swing of the reaper's scythe,
I could breathe again;
I sat in my car
Replaying the incident in my head on loop,
Thankful that I know calm, well—
Delighted in my own reflection,

Never—
Had I been so happy see to me, but
Heart broken
Because, what good is a living sacrifice
what good is my story if I never died

INSTRUMENT OF PRAISE

This body,
Is the holiest place I know;

A temple,
A tangible hallelujah,
An instrument of praise and worship;

But too often,
I feel like a question,
Like a fist full of why.
These eyes have been a witness to death.
How they turn black bodies into black holes
For all to see.

Justice, has been the best magician I've known—
How it vanishes, like black girls do

When will we know their names,

Most likely, the day we know justice

I wonder,
How safe this body really is,

Here,

It knows hate all too well.
It has seen a smile turn ravenous,
And watched bigotry foam at the mouth;

When did this world become so cold?
So afraid of the unknown,

Why does it starve for my body?
Want to swallow me whole;

It is the holiest place, I've known;

A temple

A tangible hallelujah

An instrument of praise

6 HOURS

It was the 90's—

There's a good chance,
"This is How We Do it"
Played more than 5 times
On the radio,
There's a better chance, every time
I rapped every word
Turning hand into microphone,
Passenger seat into stage
Making my dad a hype man
And all the stars an exuberant crowd

Things you learn on road trips with my father:

1: If the car stops, you use the bathroom. No matter what!
2: There is an art to changing the radio stations
3: The conversations had here will never leave you, though, they may never be repeated

Going to Alabama,
Was nothing less than everything,

All the freedom I had ever known was there;
I mean,
I had never been called nigger
Or boy there,
Never felt like all this black would get me killed
Though, I did have my first encounter with the KKK
But; I never been afraid of men who are unwilling to face the things they hate

I was,
Just too barefoot
Too shirtless
Too much of an endless sky at dusk

My father
Shed his armor,

The closer we got—
Like a weary knight after war

I,
Usually fell asleep
After, my passenger seat concerts,
The fast food, and
Father, son conversations

We arrived in Auburn like a secret
Hoping to be an unexpected surprise
It was usually late;

Funny
How the moon always found itself
Above my grandmother's house, just so

We crept up the dirt road,
Turning in her driveway,

Behold!

My grandmother in all her glory
An all-knowing sage
Stepping onto the porch,

Just as our car turned in;

"I've got some biscuits, just come out the oven"
She says,

Still,
The sweetest words ever spoken to me
Still,
The happiest I've ever been

I turned my self into a breeze that only she could embrace
I don't know that she ever let go

And when I imagine, Joy
I come to this place

To these times,

I remember the 6-hour road trips
To my grandmother's house

IF THERE BE HEAVEN

Always seance;

Answered prayer

To all—

Which was good,

Melody of

Flames

Popping Grease

Savory smoke

All

Intoxicating

Boundless smiles

Ablaze

If there be a heaven;

I pray,

It is my grandmother's kitchen

A WISE MAN

As much as I hate to admit,
My father, is a wise man,
The older I get, the more I find myself seeking his counsel;
I'm realizing, he is the only one who understands my beast;
The only who has seen his hands do,
What mine have done and survived to tell tales
My father banished his monster long ago,

Gave it job
Watched it turn into retirement;
Gave it dream too,
Watched it become a reality.

My father, is the best man I know
We talk often, our conversations short
And to the point, like the pocket knife he conceals,
Like the adamantium in his smile—

Tells me, to be the bigger man,
Smug and full himself because he knows,
He's right;
And he is,

But sometimes;
I just want permission to be a shotgun
sawed off, doubled barrel and
Black with no safety and a hair trigger, though

His wisdom, is a quiet tranquil river in the mountains
Where the air is crisp, and the wind whispers through a canopy of pine;
How it calms;
He passes perspective, like new glasses to see clearly—
Tells me, sometimes, it's better to say nothing at all,
To become the quiet,
Let action be the only sword in your arsenal—
But it's getting harder and harder these days to be silent;

I say,
Silence has become a heavy second language

I hold between my teeth,
While my name, a martyr;
Keeps spending more and more time behind my back, and

He says
They talked about Jesus—

I say
They crucified him too,

Then there was silence—
That thing I can't seem to escape,
That won't let go of neck,

I say,
What do you do,
When your bullet-proof but everyone keeps taking shots, or
When you feel like your reputation is nothing but
an ocean of rocks thrown and salt, and
Your body is the Bering Sea in winter—
Unrelenting and cold, and
Trust a talisman where my heart used to be,
My heart, a blue flame in my throat,
My mouth, a blade
Concealed like your pocket knife,
My truth defiant, sharp, and loud;
Still haven't learned to deliver it with care;
My feelings in a velvet pouch in a place only I know,
I've become more and more calloused
Like lava diving into the ocean becoming volcanic rock—

What do you do,
when being the bigger person, makes
You feel like a tight fist ready to be thrown,
And your face has become an empty mausoleum of eyes
Of beard and smile,
When all you do is hold back,
Breathe, and hold on tight to the silence—

 Again, there's that silence,
Clawing at the air—

It's interrupted by my car's frantic dinging,
'cause I never wear my seatbelt—

My father, tells me, put on your seat belt and asks—
How can you drive with that racket? and
I say I don't even hear it anymore—
he says interesting, very interesting,

And I hate,
When my father says interesting
Because usually it means,
He has made a point, and
Waiting for me to realize—

He says,
You've already learned to drown out the noise,
Explains,
He will never give me permission to be a shotgun,
I know all too well what they are capable of;
Reminds me of my monster,
Tells me to put it to work,
Give it a dream too—

Tells me,
You're right they crucified Jesus—
But, they could not stop his resurrection —

Says be that,
That force,
They will never stop.

As much as I hate to admit,

My father—

He is a wise man

MY MOTHER

My mother;
Is a talking suggestion box of question,

>She asks,
>Are you still single?
>Asks,
>When are you getting married?
>Are you dating?
>Asks,
>Are you gay?
>>Asks,
>>Are you sure?

Says, she will still love me if I am,

>She asks, when are you coming to visit?
>If I've spoken to my little brother lately?

Tells me I should;
I agree,
She calls weekly
Reminds me every time we talk,
She wants grandkids soon
Says she wants to be a young grandmother,
To this day, my mother lies about her age
Tells me to trust and believe in God,
She, embodies, the faith of a mustard seed.

My mother
Is nosey as fuck,
Has an uncanny ability to pry the secret out of you,
Our conversations have become semi-automatic
And loud like drive bys,
Our relationship is head on collision at 90 mph,
Her Christian has never seen eye to eye with my spirit,
though she prays for me daily

My mother;
Is judgmental as fuck,
Does not receive the praise she deserves,

my mother is god,
I've never known unconditional love like her,
She is a frigid tsunami of razor-sharp lotus blossoms cresting,
You can never tell if you are in imminent danger
Or on the verge of being baptized in her grace

My mother;
Is the broken home I grew up in,
She loves hard, and unconditional,
As tragic as a lonesome star in the night's sky,
She is married to the idea of a man
Who is as tangible as a blank thought,
Or a broken promise,
Who never learned the meaning of husband or father,
He loves from distance with checks
barely covering the mortgage,
She, refuses to get divorced,
Says she already made that mistake with my father
She turns water to wine with her smile and tears,
She is alone,
In a house that doesn't feel like home,
I've never known hope like hers,
Her prayers include:
Me, my brother, her marriage,
And family
Her smile has never been a high priority.

My mother,
Beat me, with

> belts,
> shoes,
> extension cords,
> broom sticks,
> Oh, and that long curly cord on the house phone,

She cried after,
I don't think she knows I saw,
She didn't beat my brother,
Didn't want to teach him that love hurts sometimes
Even though it does.
She is self-sacrifice,

Raised her sons like the full moon raises ocean tides—
She speaks in echo
Her indecipherable tone falling on def ears,
Where would I be without her sending prayers wherever I go
How, would I know my way home if it wasn't for that echo

My mother
Is tired—
She carries the weight of
Her broken heart and unanswered
prayers in a knock off handbag,
Wears Michael Kors jeans
She got on clearance and
I recently learned
She owns more shoes than I do,
Her hugs and kisses feel like apologies
For a past I never held against her—
I wonder if my hugs and kisses
Feel like an apology for not being a good son,
She answers every time I call and
She calls, though she knows I don't always answer

My mother
Is rice and beans,
Plantains with oxtails and stew chicken,
A light switch Vincentian accent and sustenance,
She's the hardest soft place I've ever known;
The epitome of,
Do as I say not as I do—
She is a hurricane in late October,
Shelter from any storm,
She is repetitive redemption and revolution, and
I've reaped from all she's sown;
My mother is my blessing,
Her eyes, a fountain of forgiveness,

For my birthday,
Every year I get a card with a check,
This year, her message read,
Hash tag— I want Grandkids

My mother

Is always with me,
she's the tears I can't seem to cry,

And this smile that won't ever go away

Credits

Self: Quote from Conversation, Dali Lama Oct 8, 2013 Atlanta, GA

Back in the Day: Excerpt- Ahmad "Back in the Day" 1994 Giant Records

6 Hours: Excerpt - Montell Jordan "This is How We Do It" 1995 Def Jam

Photo by: Jamie H.

Eean M. Tyson, known by his peers and contemporaries as Enfinite, is a man with as many skills and talents as his ambitious name implies. A global citizen and world traveler, he feels most at home on the go, always looking for a new adventure to fuel his lust for adrenaline and the passions of life. In the community of Fayetteville, North Carolina, he is a pillar in the development of the emerging art industry and is responsible for many thriving efforts in adding to the city. He's founded the Marquis Slam, a monthly poetry slam where aspiring poets come together to cultivate their craft. In addition to this, he's also started a nonprofit called Our PLACE, whose goal is to allow people more access to exercise their creativity. Ultimately, Mr. Tyson is a force to be reckoned with and his numerous escapades have made him a weary but wise storyteller. He's masterfully managed to twist his scars into epics and turn his vulnerability into something surprisingly relatable.

-Nick King

www.310brownstreet.com
@310brownstreet